moon

JOURNAL

Made in the USA
Coppell, TX
22 April 2024

31578885R00063